11 SIMPLE STEPS
TO WRITE AND PUBLISH
YOUR FIRST BOOK ON AMAZON

using a step-by-step system that will allow you to
publish many more books with ease

ANGE DOVE

Author: Ange Dove
Title: 11 Simple Steps To Write And Publish Your First Book On Amazon

Publisher: Proof Perfect Pte Ltd
81A Clemenceau Ave, #05-18, Singapore 239917

ISBN: 9798645612979
Independently published

TABLE OF CONTENTS

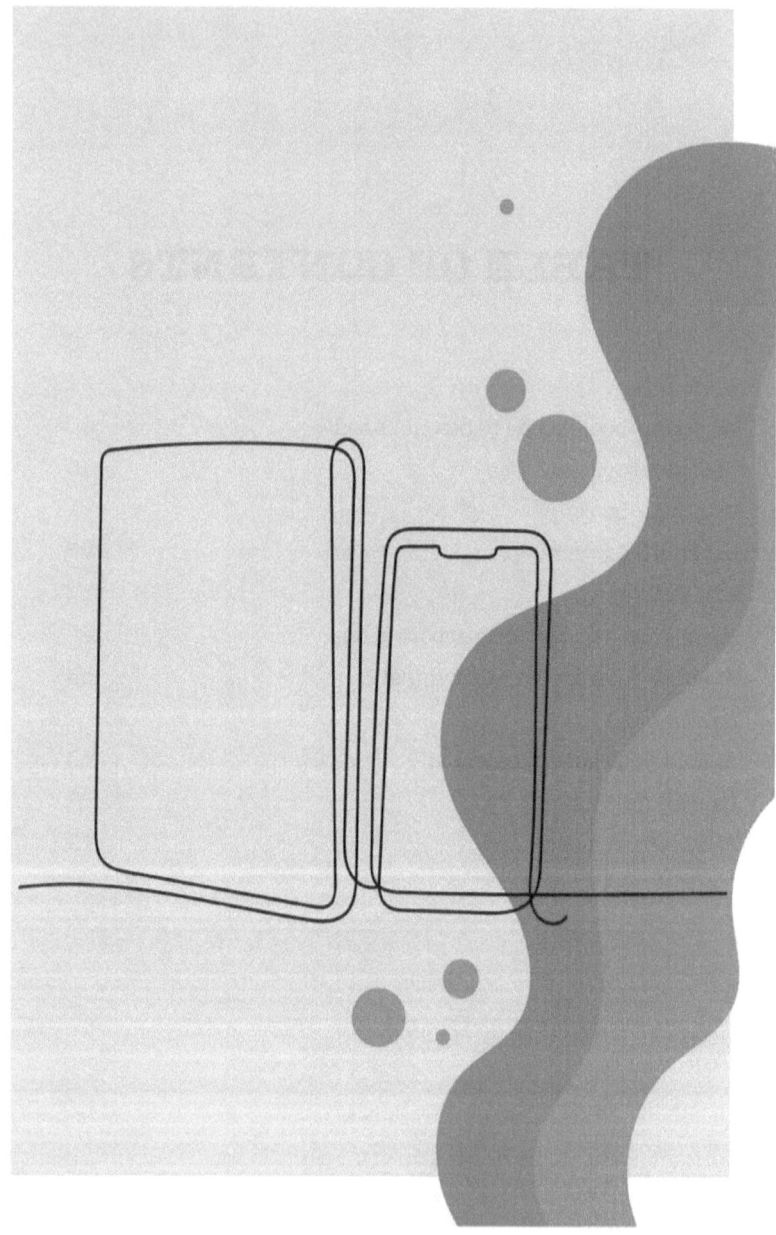

CHAPTER 1

WHY YOUR BOOK NEEDS TO BE PUBLISHED

They say everyone has a book in them. I say you've got a few in you at least! Now it's time to finally bite the bullet and get that first dream book out. Once you know the formula for doing so and you've seen your first book launch on Amazon for the world to see, I'm sure you'll find you have a host of books in you.

When I published my first book on Amazon, I did quite a few things wrong in the process and that ate into my time in a big way. But I'm glad it happened because it brought to light quite a few things that I hadn't previously learnt about publishing a book on Amazon, especially around file loading, international distribution and online promotion. Having made these mistakes, I now know what NOT to do, which is just as important as what to do. So I've been compelled to put this information into this book to make sure you don't go through the same mistakes.

If you follow the instructions in this book, it will save you so much time and heartache and you'll have your own book out and published in:

- as little as a weekend if you choose, if you can do every step yourself and you don't want to go for the best seller route
- as little as 2 months if you want to set up a promotional campaign first and implement the full best-seller strategy.

Let's get back to your story or stories. Now it's time to write yours. We've already established that you have at least one book in you - something you are an expert at that you can package into a book and help other people by shortening their learning curve as they learn quickly what it is that you know so expertly.

Your expertise is really important, and it's equally important that people get access to it. But in order to be able to get your book out, you've got to believe it's doable that you can be an author.

What's stopping you?

Perhaps this is something that's been stopping. But you have a desire to publish a book regardless. You are just blocked because you're thinking you can't be an author for whatever reason. You've got some kind of mindset block that is stopping you from writing a book because either that's something that somebody else does, or it's what famous people or "real" authors do.

I've got news for you. "Real" authors are the people who take action and get their book out there. They are no different than you. Chances are a lot of them had a professional who wrote or edited it for them. That's something you can outsource too. What can't be outsourced though is YOUR expertise. So, it's time to get over this "I can't be an author" limiting belief.

Or maybe you are thinking you can't write or you hate to write or you were no good at writing in school, so why should that have changed now?

Perhaps you just simply think that you don't have the time to write a whole book or you are questioning whether it's actually worth your time.

These thoughts are something that you're going to have to get over and this book is going to help you to surmount those blocks and realise that getting a book out is a really easy process. It's easy if you're just willing to make it a priority and go through the simple steps outlined in these chapters to get your book out of your brain, onto paper or screen and then published for the world to benefit from.

The great news is that it's something that you could literally do overnight if you were that inclined. Or at least over a weekend, and definitely over a few weeks. If you just break it down into the simple chunks I outline in this book, you can get this book out in a matter of weeks at the most.

If you want to take that long to do it, so be it, but, as I say, if you're really determined, it can be over night or over a weekend. The key is that you need to be committed to seeing it through. A lot of people start to write a book but they never finish it because they don't have a system for getting it done. They go gung-ho at the beginning and they think, *yeah, I'm going to write it* and they start to write and then, over time, the enthusiasm peters out, the desire to write wanes and they never actually get it published, or even finished.

So, I don't want that to be you. I want you to publish your book because, as I've already said, people need to hear your story. People need to hear what it is that you have to offer and you have an obligation to get that information out and share that with those who are your target audience and who need to hear it only from you.

Take action
When you think about these famous authors of bestselling books, you may wonder how your little book could possibly compete. But they all started without a book and by staring at a blank screen or page, probably thinking exactly what you are thinking right now. But they took action. That's the only difference.

They managed to get their book out and there's several ways that you can do this too, which I'm going to take you through in this book.

What's your why?
But in order to do this successfully, we really need to sort out your WHY.

Why is it that you want to write a book?

Why is it that the information that you have is so important that you need to get it out?

Why do people want or need to hear from you?

Then it becomes not about you. It becomes about them. And that's a compelling motivation to get your book out, because we rarely do things just for ourselves.

What kind of difference will writing your book make?

What difference, more importantly, would it make to the people that are going to read it?

You see, you will come to realise that actually, it's not about you. When you're writing a book or you're trying to get your message out there, you're trying to find your voice, it's not about you. It's never about you. It's never *been* about you. It's about the people that you're destined to help.

If you are still blocked right now, you are still making it about you.

So, start looking at it from the perspective of having an obligation to get this book out so that you can help people.

What other reasons could there be for writing your book? Secondary benefits include that you have your own business or you're running coaching programmes or you're some kind of expert in what you do and you want to be seen as such.

You want to be seen as the authority in your area of expertise. One way to achieve this is by becoming an author. If you think about the word "authority" and break that word down, you have "author" + "ity". Becoming an author will automatically position you as an authority and expert and people start to want to hear more from you. Your book is a sure-fire way for people to see you as an expert without you even having to prove it in any other way. It's simply assumed that because you have a book, you must be an authority. Of course, you must deliver the value to back that up at some point!

Another reason that a book is good for you and good for your business is that it can be the best name card you've ever had. Imagine that you're meeting someone for the first time and they are a potential customer or you need to be able to convey to this person that you are the person for the job, that you should be hired, that they should do business with you.

Imagine the difference between giving out a name card which just gives your position and contact details and doesn't really say an awful lot more about you or your business or what it is that you do, and instead you give them your book. That is an automatic credibility boost, an automatic credibility builder right there. It's much better than a name card. So think about that next time you're giving out your name card. Wouldn't it be great if you could give them a book instead?

These are all secondary benefits to getting your book out. Let's face it, mastery alone is not enough. You need to find your main why, your main purpose and driver for writing a book. We've established that a book is a great vehicle to use to build your credibility, expertise and authority. Now you want to be able to see the process through and remove any of those limiting beliefs that have stopped you so far.

And if you have a strong enough why to deliver your book to the world, nothing's going to stop you from doing it. So you really need to understand your why, the reason driving you.

It should not be about the money. First of all, selling a book is not going to make you rich. You can make money in ways that are a lot easier than writing and self-publishing a book, so don't make it about the money.

You've got to be thinking about putting your book out as a way to perpetuate your brand to make you stand out, to make you an authority in your niche. Having a book will help you gain respect and make you credible to people that don't yet know you well.

If you make it about the money and you're only in it for the money, you're not going to succeed in anything you do in the long run by writing a book.

You can if you think you can
Have we cleared those blocks that have stopped you from writing a book in the past? Let's get rid of that last niggling doubt. If you think you can or you think you can't, you're right. This is a classic quote attributed to Henry Ford and it's a very true statement of fact really. *If you think you can or you think you can't you're right* seems a confusing statement. You can't be right thinking both ways. Right? One of them should be right and one wrong. But actually the key word here is "think".

If you think you can, you can. If you think you can't, well then you can't. It's all mindset. If you believe that you can write this book then I'm 100% certain that you can write this book.

Take it step by step

The book that you're reading right now is going to teach you how to write your book by following an easy, step-by-step system. So just remember that you can decide how you think. You can decide what's possible. You can decide to do this.

Well, that kind of sums up the reason why you should write this book and how to remove the blocks that have stopped you from doing so thus far. If you think about it in terms of what your readers are going to gain from it, if you think about what your business and personal brand is going to gain from it in terms of the prestige, the authority, the credibility, if you think of how your personal brand can be developed because of your book, these are much better motivators for you to write a book than simply the money.

You are here to make a difference to the people who want to learn from you. You're going to contribute to their knowledge bank. You may contribute to changing the trajectory of their lives even. But you're certainly going to be able to help them in some way with what you know.

So let's get writing your book!

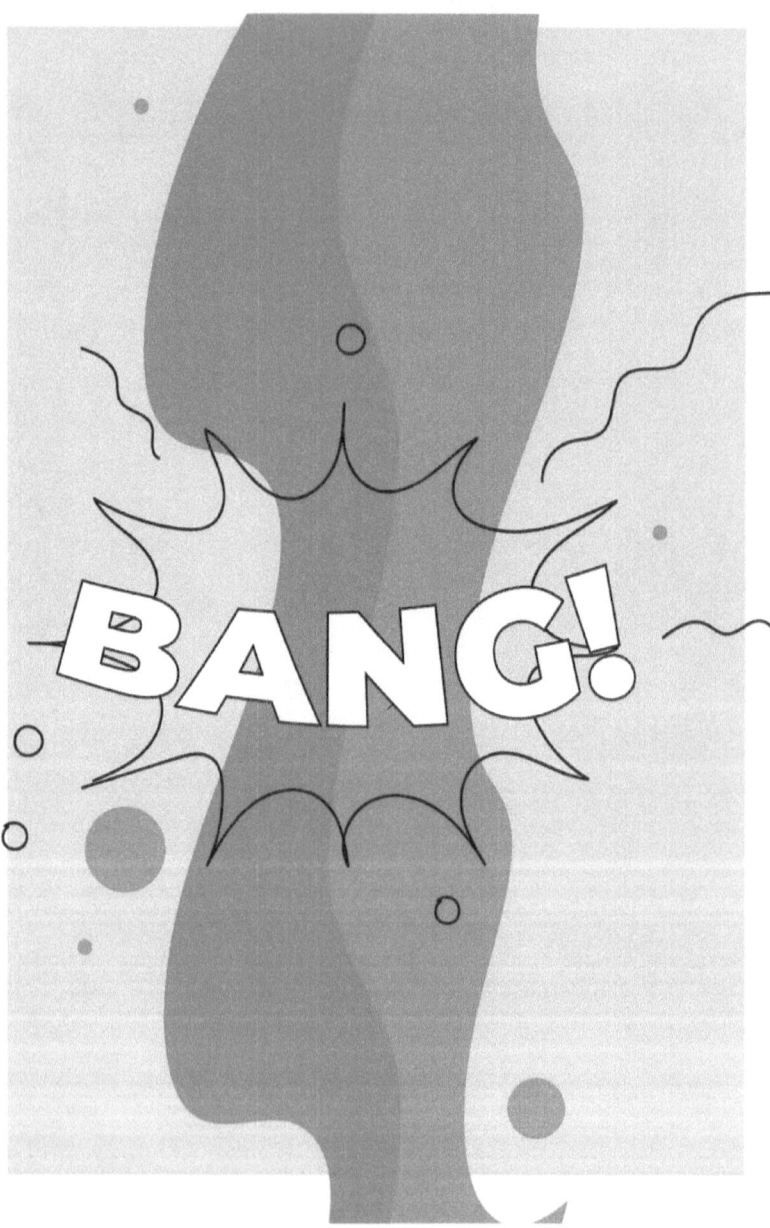

CHAPTER 2

CHOOSE A TOPIC
AND TITLE

Let's get right down to choosing the topic for you book and its title. When you choose a title for a book, it's got to be something that hooks the attention of your reader straight away. You know yourself when you're in a bookstore browsing the shelves that how the cover looks makes you pick up a certain book. It may be the colours in the design that first grab your attention. But the thing that's going to make you pick it up and open it is the title. What is the title that you're going to give your book?

Your title needs to scream attention
Your title is the thing that's going to make people take it off the bookshelves. It's the thing that's going to make people who see it advertised online be immediately attracted to it. It's what's going to make them, when they go to Amazon, decide to buy it.

As you can see, your title is really important. Yes, it has to scream attention. But more than that, it has to really sell the benefit or offer a solution to a problem. So your title needs to make it really clear that your book is going to address a certain problem that the reader has and it's going to solve that problem for them. Your reader is going to find the answers to their problem or how to solve that problem in your book.

Test your title ideas

Just a word of warning on choosing your title. You may have a title already in mind now, but I'd advise you to keep an open mind. Don't commit completely to that title. Be open to other titles that might crop up. Be open-minded to other suggestions that other people might suggest for you because they can see things maybe a little bit clearer than you can. It's always good to get a few points of view. Sometimes we are too close to it to be objective.

So test your title by putting it out maybe on Facebook in a poll or something like that or in one of your social groups that are made up of people that are your target audience. You can ask them to test it out for you. Give them several different titles and see which one most people resonate with. At least it will give you pause for thought and set you in the right direction. If there is an obvious preference, it will have been worth the effort to test. If you get a clean split, then use your gut feeling. Which version resonates the most with you?

How to create a good title to test

It needs to have a promise in it. It needs to give the impression that the book is going to help the reader and in some way solve a particular problem that they have. If you are completely blank, browse the Amazon bookstore and look at the titles of other books. Select the categories that you would put your book into to see what kind of titles are out there. If your book is about business, you want to be looking through the business categories. If your book is on Business Finance, then you want to go into the Business category and then look under the Finance category within the Business category. There are certain niches that you can really drill down into and then look at the books that are there. Look at those books because they're going to be your competitors in a way. You're going to be competing against them for sales. So you want to look at what's already out there and you want to look at what's missing in terms of what's not being addressed on the bookshelf that you see on Amazon. How can your book add value by giving some information that maybe is not really being adequately addressed with the currently published collection. You can also do this research if you have no clue about what topic to cover at all.

Formatting the title

Once you have your topic, you need to be looking at the way to write the title. What do you notice about the titles you see on other books? You'll notice that most contain two parts. You'll see that you'll have a main title obviously, but there's usually a subtitle that will give the details of what the book is really about.

The main title should give enough information to give an idea of what the book is about but it can also create intrigue and have a hook that will raise curiosity. The title really has got to be that commanding promise, but your subtitle then drills down into the full explanation. That's going to clinch it for the reader and have them say *yes, this is the book. This is what I'm thinking this book is about so I will buy it because I know from this subtitle that it is the book that I want to read.*

Notice that titles will be short and subtitles can be longer. The title could be promising *How to..* or offer *7 steps to..* or it could start with an action word. Look at the bestsellers. Model your title structure on any of these as they've obviously done something right.

This kind of in-depth research is a good way to choose your book topic, title and subtitle. Be openminded as to what this research brings up for you rather than just going with your first thought. You might be surprised at how your thoughts can change once you see what else is out there. Go and do the research.

People do judge a book by its cover, so putting time into what's on the cover is a good investment of your own time and it's something you will want to get right so that you can command the attention of potential readers.

CHAPTER 3

PLAN
YOUR BOOK

In this chapter, we're going to look at how you can plan out the contents of your book. As the famous saying goes, if you fail to plan, you plan to fail. You don't want to fail in writing your book. You want it to be a great bestseller if you can achieve that, or at least it's something that people will want to read and they'll get value out of. So you don't want to just write anything that comes to mind. You need to plan it out carefully

How do you plan to write a book?

Create a skeleton
The first thing you want to do is map out a skeleton plan of the book, your contents page if you like.

Start by listing main sub topics that come under the main topic of your book. Just list out as many ideas as you can think of in this brainstorming session without censoring yourself. No idea is good or bad. Just got it down on paper.

For example, if I'm writing a book on how to build a marketing funnel, I might want to include a chapter about how to place an ad because that'll be the first step of the marketing funnel. Then I'll want to create a chapter on what makes a good lead or the hook that gets people to give their email to me. I might want to create a chapter all about how to do a webinar as a choice of sales page within the funnel, etc.

So you just want to break up the sub topics and list them down.

Next, narrow and combine these topics into between seven and 11 main sub topics. Any less than seven, you probably won't have content long enough for a decent book. Anything more than 11 and probably it's just too much information for your reader to be able to cope with. So keep it within that range of seven to 11 chapters. You could do it as *7 great reasons why* ... or *9 ways to* ... Think about some of the successful books that are out there like Seven Habits of Highly Successful People and books like that. You will notice that a lot of these books tend to have odd numbers in the title.

Once you are happy that these sub-topics complete your book, organise the list into a logical order, especially if your book offers a step-by-step system like this book does. There would be no good my teaching you how to publish your book before you've written it.

Now you have your contents page and chapter titles decided upon!

Flesh out each idea

Next, take each of these chapter topics and brainstorm once again, this time what sub topics should be included within each chapter and then organise these into order. That's the whole skeleton to your book!

You can go into the details of naming your chapters properly later when you get into the editing phase. For now the skeleton you have is all you need to get going with writing your book. And once you've done that process, you've actually done the hardest part of publishing a book, to be honest. I hope that this process provides you with a sense of relief, a sense that yes, this is going to be possible now that you have a structure. Now it's all about fleshing it out. And that's OK because you will be writing about what you know.

You can now see the book actually being finished because you know what's going to go into it in terms of its general structure. It's a great place to start writing your book. And the other good thing about this is that now you're not actually writing a book, in a way. You are kind of writing a shorter essay multiplied by the number of chapters in your book. That's doable.

Now you've broken the book up into manageable pieces, you can tackle one by one. It now suddenly becomes much more manageable. When you first started out thinking that you wanted to write a book, your mind, thinking about a book of many, many pages, considered it to be an almost insurmountable task. *How am I going to manage to write 100 pages of a book or 200 pages of a book? How am I going to do this? It just seems like it's going to go on forever and it's a really difficult task.* But once you have set it out into these subtopics, all you have to do is focus on one topic at a time rather than a whole book. And that's what we're going to focus on in the next chapter. Let's get started on writing your book.

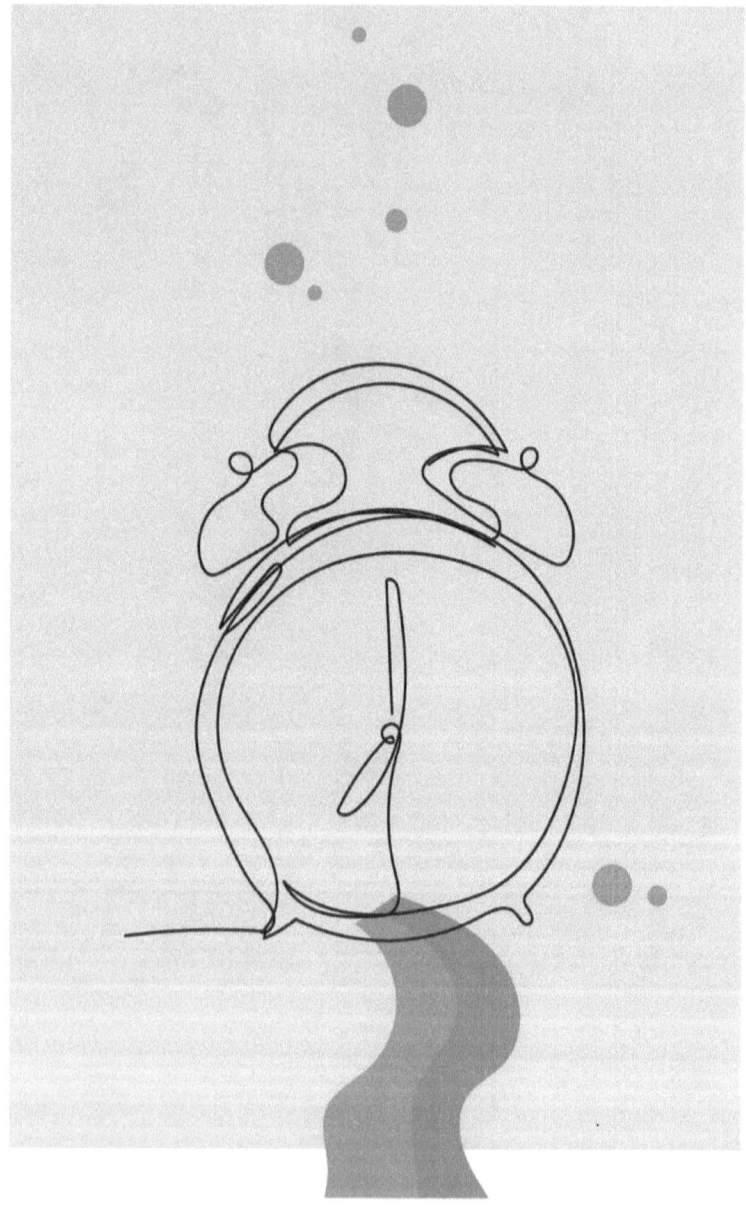

CHAPTER 4

SCHEDULE
THE WRITING

The great thing about starting to write your book is that you are going to take it one easy chapter at a time. You no longer have to look at it as a whole book anymore, for now. Not until it's written anyway.

Work on a chapter at a time
So avoid looking at the book as a whole anymore because then, you're never going to get it finished. Just tackle the one chapter at a time. Don't try to work on multiple chapters at the same time either. Just work on one chapter at a time.

Here's what's going to make it even easier. You don't need to start at chapter 1 and progress chronologically. Each chapter is independent of one another so you can start ANYWHERE. Just start with the one chapter you feel you have the most to talk about, the easiest one for you, the one that you think that the information is going to flow really easily because it's really easy for you to be able to communicate the ideas to your target reader.

Just start with the easiest chapter because, once you make a start, then it's going to be easier to continue, whereas if you're just staring at a blank page and you never make a start, your book is definitely not going to get written.

The writing process
There are several ways that you can get your book out into the written form.

If you are a person that does actually like writing or you like typing, one of the ways you can start is to take that easiest chapter, say it's Chapter 4. So, take chapter 4, take the subtopics you listed and make sure they are listed in a logical order for logical flow and will be logical for completing that chapter. This will now be your checklist for completing the chapter.

Now get to that word processing software, such as Microsoft Word or Google Docs, on your computer and just start typing away.

Work with that first sub topic and start to write about it. Now at this stage, don't try to make it a good book. Don't try to make it perfect. Don't try to make it the best seller you may want it to be. Don't be critical on what is coming out onto the page either. Just type away. Just keep going until it's done. Get all your ideas from your brain onto the page without any filter whatsoever. Do not, under any circumstances, go back and correct any spelling errors or typing errors. Do not be critical on the way that you phrased a certain sentence. Just get everything down without really looking at what you're typing. Just type it out and get the ideas onto the page in some format. That is a starting place for you to craft that chapter into something really good later on.

Your task at this first stage of the writing process is just to get the information out from your brain onto the page without any editing, without any filtering, without any worry about what kind of quality it is. We are not looking at quality right now. We are looking at just getting the information out onto the page so that we have something to work with.

Now, if you don't like writing, what you can do instead is download a dictation app onto your phone and dictate the chapter into the phone. I use Live Transcribe and find it very accurate. Apply the same principle as I have just described for typing out your story but dictate it instead. Don't filter, or stop and go back and correct. Just dictate and talk until you have nothing more to add. The editing process later will sort the rest out.

Does this really work? you may ask. This is the way I've written this book. I simply spoke all the information I wanted to have in the book into the app on my mobile phone. The words you speak fill the screen and keep going until you stop speaking. You can speak your whole chapter in a matter of minutes!

When you have finished dictating, simply save the text in the app. Next select all text and copy it. Then open up a Word or Google document on your phone and paste the text into it. Then upload that file into your Dropbox or Google Drive or whatever file storage system you use.

On your main computer, you can retrieve the text you have saved and start to separate it into clear chapters and put it all together into one document as you complete each chapter. This will get your text, your whole book, ready for the editing process, which is where you will begin to mould this rough first draft into the eventual final draft of your book.

Planning your time

Before you begin the typing or dictating process though, you need to decide on your timeframe to get the book completed. How you choose to do that depends really on your character, your preference and the amount of time you have to do this in and how much of a priority you're going to make it.

You could do the same as how I did this book. I dictated it into my phone on a Friday evening and pasted the text into a Word document.

The next morning I organised all my chapters and made sure I had pasted in all texts that I had dictated.

Then I used the Saturday afternoon and evening to edit the text into better constructed thoughts and sentences.

On the Sunday, I printed and proofread the whole book and made my final changes.

On the Monday I sent the brief to my illustrator to create the illustrations that divide each chapter.

Once I got those back a few days later, I added them into my Word document in the places I wanted them and I added the front page matter.

You can do your book in a block of time like this over the weekend, or you could take a bit more time with it and decide to do a chapter a day. So you could map out maybe two hours every day to complete each chapter. Maybe every morning when you get up, you could spend two hours dictating the chapter into your phone, or you could do a chapter a week and just concentrate on maybe a couple of minutes each day, just doing a little bit of the chapter each time.

However, I would recommend doing no fewer than one chapter a week because if you're going to do nine chapters, for example, that's going to be nine weeks. For me, that's quite a long process just to get the first draft out. But, you know yourself. You know what you can commit to doing. I would say the sooner you can do it or just get that first draft out, the easier it will be to keep the momentum going.

Whichever way you decide to tackle this, whether you decide to do it in a day, in a weekend, in a week, or in nine weeks, whatever timetable you set for yourself, make a commitment that you're going to write your book and you're going to stick to that timetable so that at the end of the scheduled time, you have your first rough draft all written out and ready to go.

Set a timetable

Once you've agreed with yourself on a completion date for the first draft, it would be good to set a timetable now for the entire completion of all stages of getting the book written, edited and published.

The timeframe you give yourself and the number of steps you need to timetable will depend on your goal for the book.

If you simply want to write and publish the book, you will be plotting much fewer steps than if you want to employ the strategy I will detail later in this book to attempt to become a number 1 bestseller on Amazon.

Here are the stages you need to plan for:

Write and publish only	Write and publish to attempt to be an Amazon bestseller
Write each chapter	Put out teaser on your book plan
Edit the book to improve sentence structure and content	Gather interest and create a launch support group
Edit for grammar, spelling and punctuation	Create landing page and WhatsApp group
Lay out book	Write and upload an email automation for the promotion of the book to your interested list
Editing of layout for consistency	Consider ads to drive additional traffic
Proofreading final draft in layout	Write each chapter
Upload to Kindle Create and format	Edit the book to improve sentence structure and content
Upload to KDP and publish	Edit for grammar, spelling and punctuation
If uploading a paperback version, submit to KDP for file approval	Lay out book
Put final book file live	Editing of layout for consistency
	Proofreading final draft in layout
	Give book to select people for review
	Keep promoting to your platforms with your collected reviews
	Upload to KDP at least 3 weeks before launch date and select the launch date
	Keep promoting to your lists for 3 weeks
	Activate the bestseller launch strategy on the launch date
	Launch KDP ads

Be accountable

Be aware of the planning process in terms of when you're going to get your final book out, commit to the date when your book is going to be completely ready by and available on Amazon. Commit to that date by writing out a little contract to yourself pledging that you'll see this book through to completion. Print out this contract, sign it and have it witnessed by someone who is going to be your accountability partner in this process.

Your accountability partner will hold you accountable for you getting your book done by the date you have committed to. This will be useful only if you actually advise that person of your milestone dates for each section needed to get the book out. Share your full timetable so that they understand what is involved and what you must finish by what date.

Get those details fully organised so that you're going to stay on track with the book and you're not going to leave it aside and come back to it two years later to publish it! You don't want to go down that road.

You should feel even more compelled to complete your book now that you have a plan of the content, a clear timetable for completion and an accountability partner to hold you accountable for getting it done.

Remember that, at this stage, you are not looking for perfection. You're not looking for anywhere near perfect. You are just aiming to get the information into a document for you to be able to work on.

Now that you have your draft saved into a Word document, you are going to work on making it next to perfect. Not perfect mind, as it will never be. If you set perfect as your goal, I promise you that you will never publish the thing. Forget perfect. Good enough will be enough.

The next stage of the process is going to be the main hard work, I will be honest. Depending on your personality profile, you are either going to find this next stage of the process very laborious or you'll be in your element! Either way, it has to be done.

This is where your inner critic gets to SHINE!

But there is a process to doing this part of the work too.

Complete the writing phase

In your first draft, there are bound to be many, many spelling errors and funny turns of phrase. If there aren't, then you didn't do the previous stage correctly! Writing and editing are two very different processes and should never be combined. Let your creative juices flow in the writing stage and let your inner critic reign in the separate editing phase that comes after.

Firstly, you are going to need to flesh out some of the information and make it a bit more logical or understandable in some way because as you dictated or typed earlier, you were not really planning what you were communicating. You were in flow but not perfect.

Now, you're going to look really critically at what came out of your head and rewrite it into something that reads a lot more planned, a lot more sophisticated. This is where you are really starting to put the book together in a way that makes sense and it's readable. That's your next stage.

So, set yourself time to go through each chapter individually, working to your planned timetable and improve on the writing so that you're more or less happy with what you've got there as a final written draft in the writing process. It should be something that you think people are going to be quite happy to read in terms of the content, the information you are sharing.

Don't worry yet about the grammar, spelling and punctuation and all that kind of stuff. Focus just on the content, the valuable information that you're imparting. Just make sure that this is coming out in the way that you want it to be read, in the order that you want it to be read and that it makes sense in the way that it is portrayed, structured and ordered.

Finally, you are done with the writing process!

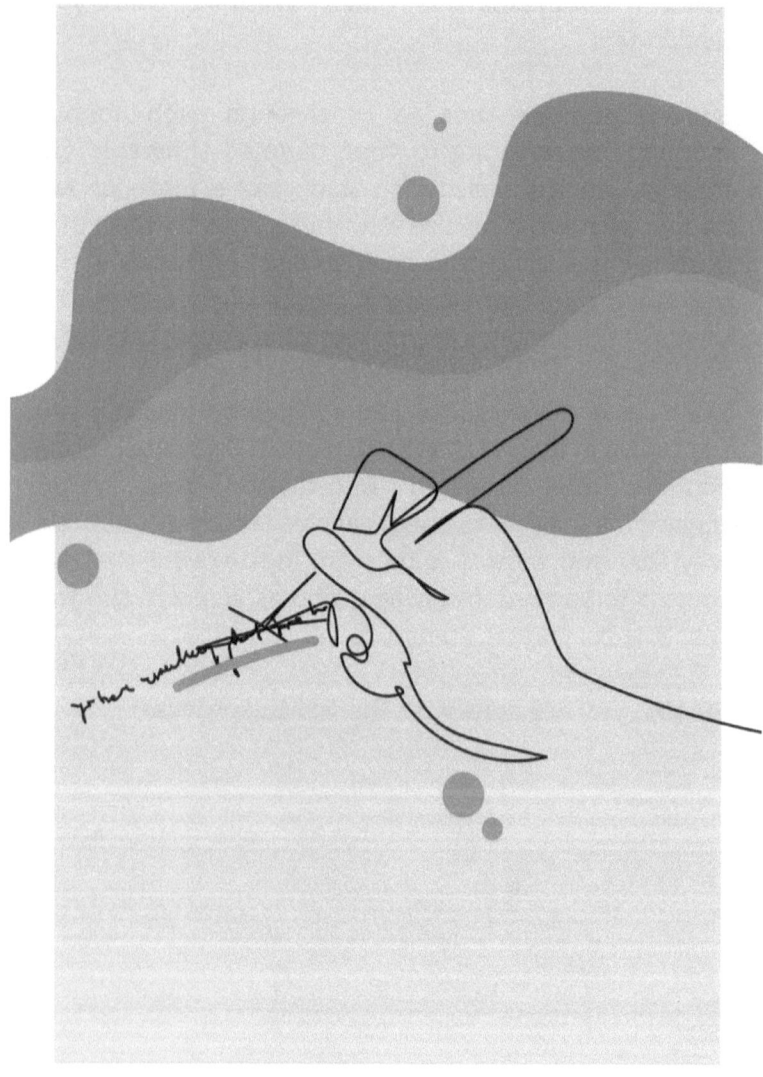

CHAPTER 5

EDIT RUTHLESSLY

Congratulations! You have finished the writing process and you have essentially written a book. But it's not quite time to celebrate just yet!

Now is the time for the editing process so that you can turn what you have written into something that is publishable. At the moment, it's for your eyes only! Only you want it to be read by the public, so it is going to need to be edited.

Assign an editor
The first thing to decide is whether you want to do this yourself or pay a professional editor to do it for you.

I would suggest that you make a decision based on your ability to write something coherent. We're not all great writers. So it depends on your individual talents. You will know yourself your own ability. Decide whether you are good enough at writing to be able to edit the book that you've written yourself or whether you need to hire a professional editor to do it for you.

If you are confident in your use of the written language, you're a good writer and you know you are, you will be able to edit the book yourself. Just leave some time away from the book before you attempt to edit it so that you are coming to it with a fresh pair of eyes. But only edit it yourself if you can be critical with what you wrote. If there are any darlings in there that you won't be able to remove even if it doesn't serve the book, then outsource this process to an editor who can be impartial.

Rephrasing

If you do decide to go ahead with the editing yourself, be critical with yourself and really analyse whether what you have written at each stage actually makes sense. Can you rephrase to make it read better? Look at long sentences and see how they can be trimmed. Does the content have a logical flow? Will your readers be confused at any point? If your text raises questions, it should be reworded.

Sentence structure

Have you included a nice mix of different types of sentence structures and lengths so that it has a rhythm when it's read? You don't want it all staccato short sentences. That's annoying to read. But you don't want it so that you have all long sentences either because your reader will give up on trying to read it. So you want to look at those kind of things: your sentence structure, how to make it interesting and a good read for your audience.

Layout

Another thing you need to look at in the editing process is the layout of the information. A lot of people don't like to read books that are completely laid out in prose with no or few paragraph breaks and no sub headings to break up the information. A lot of readers nowadays have not got the patience to read long texts and they'll be completely put off. To write a good book that is going to be a quick and easy read for your audience, you want to be thinking about putting subheadings into your chapters. This makes it easy for your readers to scan through and see what the topics are about and whether that information will be relevant to them.

Redundancies

Next you need to go back and reread again and be very critical on whether you have used any redundant words. Are you saying the same thing over and over again? Are you boring your reader? Are you using words repetitively and as you read it through, you start to notice the same words coming up? You need to start to ramp up your vocabulary at that stage and replace some of those repetitive words.

Have you included words that just aren't really needed? For example, saying something is "very unique". You don't need the word "very" because "unique" by definition is absolute. There is no being "slightly unique" or "very unique", it's just "unique".

Look at words like "also" as well. This is a common word that is overused. Look for other words you tend to overuse and cut them out of your book in the editing process.

Be very critical of rambling. Which words can you cut and still communicate the same thing but much more concisely and crisply? You need to cut out I would say probably 30% of your text at the very least in the editing process. It will improve the readability of the book no end. Your reader will thank you for it.

By cutting, you will be making your book a lot crisper and easier for your readers to consume rather than boring them with long laborious sentence structures and words that are just not needed. Make your points succinctly.

Grammar, spelling and punctuation

Next you want to focus on the grammar, spelling and punctuation. Because you are dealing with a long book rather than a short article, the editing process can get quite involved. You will find yourself looking up the same words in the dictionary over and over to make sure you are using the correct form if you don't have a system in place to avoid this. Let me give you an example. Say you have used the word "post office" a lot in your book and in some places it is "post office", in others it is "post-office" and in others it is "postoffice". You need to use the correct form and use it consistently throughout the book. If you don't have a system, you'll find that you can't remember in chapter 8 what you had agreed on in Chapter 2 and you'll need to refer to the dictionary again even though you've already been through this once or even a few times.

Vocabulary sheet

To avoid this, create a record sheet for uncertain words. Do this by creating a table of 10 boxes on one piece of paper, and 10 on another and another six boxes on the third piece of paper. Label each box with a letter of the alphabet in alphabetical order. Each time you come across a problem word that you're not quite sure about and you need to look up in the dictionary, pop the correct version of the word into the right box - e.g. your "post office" word will be placed in the P box. Next time the word comes up in your text, you simply have to refer to this vocabulary sheet. You may *think* that you don't need to do this, but you'll find that, as you are going through, if you don't do it, I promise you, you're going to be going back to the dictionary for the same word several times and it's going to get really irritating. So take my advice and create this word list so that you can easily and quickly deal with problem words and keep them consistent throughout the book.

Next, one by one, do a Find command search in your document for every word you have written on your list to check that you have each word used consistently and you didn't miss any out.

Set your document language

Another thing that you need to take note of, and this is something to do at the very beginning of your editing process, is to set the language for the document. Are you going to use UK or US English? Once this is set, look at every word that Word has underlined in red and fix the spelling errors. For example, if you select to use UK spelling but you have used the word "center" throughout, Word will flag this as a wrong spelling. A word of caution though, if you are deciding to do your book in the UK language and you want to have all your words spelled with an S instead of Z (as in "organisation" and not "organization"), Word will not flag words spelled in the Z form as being wrong. You will have to comb through manually to make those changes.

Comma use

Another common error in writing is misuse of the comma punctuation. If you are not sure of the rules, either learn them or hire an editor to check for you. Be aware too that the rules for comma use are very different in US English as compared to UK English.

If you are comma savvy, go through your book and make sure that you have put your commas in the right places. Generally speaking, a comma will indicate a pause for breath. So, where you would naturally pause for breath in speaking, you would put a comma. Commas are also placed if there is a possibility of your sentence being taken either of two ways. A comma will help to make your intended meaning clear.

The other rule they say is "if in doubt leave it out". So, err on the side of not over punctuating your text with commas, but know where they should go. You don't want to leave a comma out if it's going to confuse the reader or give a different meaning to your sentence. As I say, if you're not sure about this then the best thing to do is to hire a professional editor to do it for you. But you need to make sure that you get an editor familiar with the right style. If you're writing in the UK language, your editor needs to be aware of the common rules for the particular language choice that you're making.

Consistency of layout

When it comes to you having the book laid out, you need to go through the editing process again in the laid-out version of your book to make sure the design is consistent throughout.

You will be checking that your chapter titles all have the same font and font size and the same goes with the sub-headers. Check the text hierarchy (H1, H2, H3, etc.) is consistent all the way through the book.

Check too that the page numbers flow and that the Contents page references the correct page numbers and that the chapter names in the Contents page match the chapter names in each chapter.

So that's it really about the editing process.

Proofreading
Next comes the proofreading process. Once you've got the book out in its laid-out format, you need to go through a final check to look for any unspotted typos. The reason for this final check is that, by this time, you have read your book so many times, you have become kind of word blind to certain errors and you just don't see them anymore because you've read it so many times. In addition, the brain tends to compensate for errors so they go completely unnoticed. You've probably seen the example of the double "the" in a piece of text where the two "the" words are separated by a line break. One "the" appears at the end of one line and the other "the" starts the next line. It's very likely that you would not notice the extra "the" and would read the sentence "correctly" but not as it has been wrongly written!

So proofreading is quite tricky because your brain, as you're reading something (especially if it's interesting and it makes sense to you), switches off its checking process and doesn't notice the errors. For this reason, you need to manage your proofreading process in a very structured way and give yourself plenty of breaks and allow yourself a lot of time.

What I would suggest also is that you do not proofread on the same day as you edit. Leave it aside for a few days at least or try to give it a week. If you can, give it longer before you go and do the final proofreading. This way, when you come back to it, you'll be looking at it with a fresh pair of eyes and you'll be able to see things that you couldn't see before because you had become so blind to the errors.

More "hands" make light work

Now, even though you do this and you can catch a lot of errors doing it this way, I highly advise that you hire a professional proof reader to go through the final draft to lend a completely fresh pair of eyes. They will be in a much better position to be able to see typos that you haven't spotted. I would also suggest that you give out the book to a few of your friends and get them to read it. Ask each of them to come back to you with any errors that they've spotted as well. So that way you can be quite sure that you've more or less spotted most of the errors when you get quite a few different pairs of eyes looking at that final draft.

Once you've collated all of the feedback, go in and make the final change to your script. But a word of warning here: What you want to really be careful with, when you do that final bit of editing in putting in those final changes, is that you don't create an extra mistake when you're removing the highlighted mistake. For example, if you were changing the word order and you add a word in a different place in the sentence and forget to remove the same word from its original place, you will end up with that word in the sentence twice. So, be careful when you are making those corrections that you make them very carefully. You don't want to add final errors into the final draft where there were none before.

Finally, add in the front matter to your book: the copyright and publishing statements and the dedication and foreword pages if you have them.

Your book is done. Now let's get it published!

CHAPTER 6

FORM YOUR LAUNCH SUPPORT GROUP

Before we cover the procedure for uploading and launching your book on Amazon, I want to go over the book launch strategy for if you do want to try to become a best-seller.

In this chapter, I will discuss how to form your launch support group, get some testimonials that will support the marketing of your book before you launch it, and prep your audience for the upcoming planned future launch.

What is a launch support group?

If you want to be an Amazon bestseller, having a steady stream of buyers on launch day puts you in a stronger position to reach the number 1 spot in your category.

If you can get 200 people agreeing to support your launch, this should be enough. But assuming not all will cooperate or be available on the day, you would be wise to build a larger group if you can.

This group will need to be there for you on launch day and, upon your instruction, will go in and buy a copy of the book on the day that you launch it. If you don't care about being a bestseller, you can ignore this stage.

But if you do want to attempt to be a best-seller, then you need to have a launch team that's going to support your launch on the day of launch. And there is a certain process that you need to follow in order to create that buzz to get the buying done on the day of launch so that you can become a best-seller in your category. Being a best-seller is not a guarantee as it depends how many people buy, how many other books are selling on the same day in the same category and how competitive the category is.

So what is the strategy?
1. Well, you need to create your launch support group first and well ahead of your launch date, preferably about 6 weeks beforehand.
2. Start to create a buzz on your social media accounts, your communities and your lists. Put the message out there that you are in the process of writing a book and create some excitement around it.
3. You can publish posts that show your cover design when you've got it out.
4. You can even bring your group into the design process by asking them to vote for one of a selection of designs.
5. You can show posts that talk about the process you are going through writing the book.
6. You could give them a first chapter just as a teaser to say, Hey, this is the first chapter of my book. If you're interested, let me know and I'll give you the details for when it launches, etc.

7. You can show illustrations of the book day by day.
8. You can bring people to a strong landing page from a Facebook ad to have them register for a pre order of your book and get them into your list.

Each day, just post something that raises some kind of excitement for the book.

You want to follow these eight strategies to create some excitement among your audience about the book that's coming. Get them excited for the launch date.

Build a list
Once you've got people organically interested, you want to lead them to the same landing page you have created for your ad where you capture their emails in exchange for a free chapter of the book, or ask them to sign up to pre-register for the book ready for when it comes out. Explain to them that they will be notified when the book is available.

You now have a list of interested parties that have committed to being your launch support team. You can send regular emails to them to keep them updated and interested and increase the frequency and excitement the closer you get to launch day.

Another strategy that you can use which is very useful is to create a WhatsApp group or a Telegram group and keep people up-to-date on the process of your book via those mediums as well as via email.

Whichever communication medium you choose, you need to be able to communicate to your launch support group regularly about the process that you're going through, and make it very clear when your launch date is coming up and what you need them to do and when.

You need to give clear instructions as to what you want them to do in order to make your book a best-seller. So, you need to get them to agree that they will go and buy the book on the launch day at this ridiculously discounted price of 99 US cents.

This pre-launch build-up is one of the processes that you need to have in place before you launch your book. This is why you need that six-week lead-up.

The importance of pre-launch reviews

Get positive reviews of your book before the launch so that you can market how great the book is. To do this, provide about 10 people with the whole book for them to review. They get the book for free in exchange for a positive review. Just be clear with them that they only need to provide a review if they feel they can be positive about the book. You don't want to bribe anyone!

Use these reviews as social proof that people are saying *I've read the book and it's really good.*

Now let's get onto how to conduct your teaser campaigns to drum up interest in your book before it goes on sale.

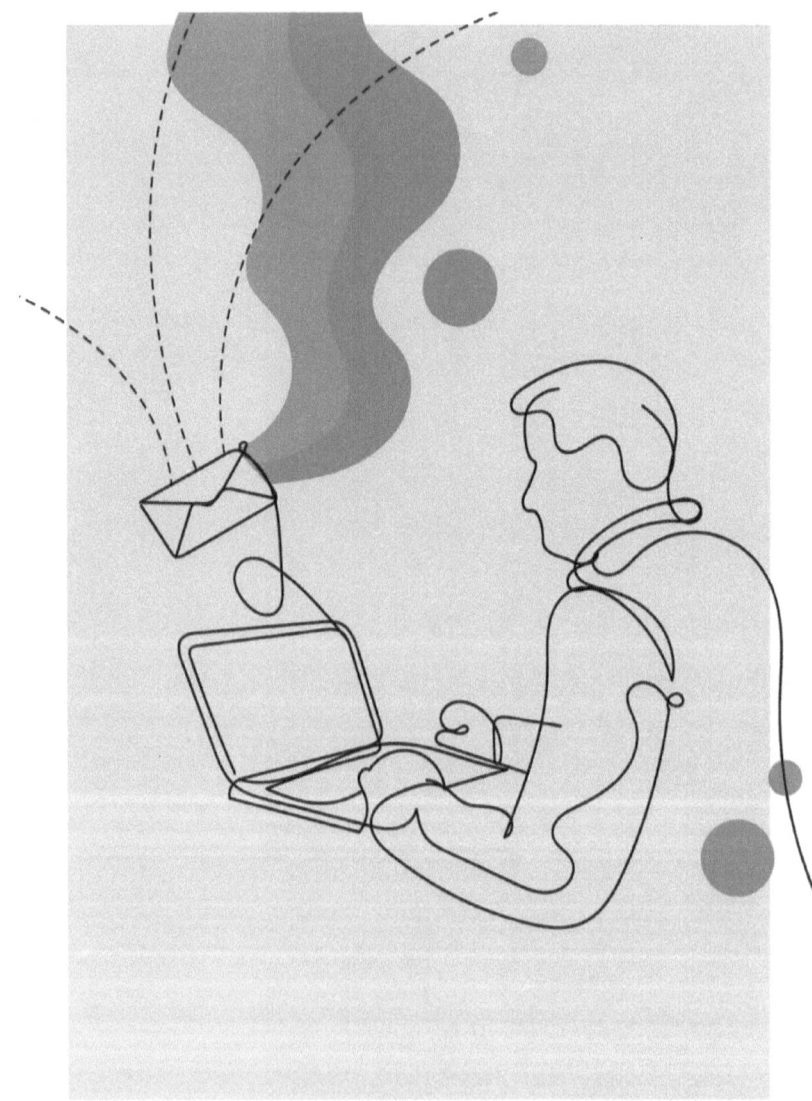

CHAPTER 7

EXECUTE YOUR PRE-LAUNCH CAMPAIGN

In this chapter, I will be looking at how to create your teaser campaigns to drum up interest in your book in the pre-launch phase beyond your initial support group. So as I mentioned earlier, you need to be drumming up interest for at least six weeks before your launch date if you are implementing the best-seller strategy. So be coming up with regular content about your book until you get to the point where it sticks with people. You will know that has happened when you get people commenting that they know you are releasing a book.

Basically, you need to make sure everybody knows that this book is coming out and you need to be putting out teaser content on a regular basis.

Picture posts
Put out daily posts that show what your book is going to look like in little teaser increments. This can be a snapshot of an inside page, the cover, the back cover, a sequence of illustrations teased out one per day, any images you have in the book, etc.

Video teachings

Record short 1-2 minute videos of you talking about a key topic in your book. You could do one of these per day for the last 10 days leading up to launch day. At the end of each video, plug the book and send them to the landing page to pre order.

Build to fever pitch

Ramp up the frequency and the fever pitch the nearer to the launch date you get. You can start with a casual announcement to say *Hey, I'm writing a book and this is what it's about* and give them a little bit of insight into it. Then as the weeks progress closer to your launch, you need to be making that communication more frequent, ramping up into the last week before the launch, where your posts are going to be several times a day.

Teasing the launch of my first book, I put out quite a lot of posts up around showing the illustrations that were in the book and garnered interest that way. People became a bit curious about the visuals that they were seeing and why these were being shown.

I also recorded short one-minute videos with a teaching point for each chapter of the book to garner more interest. Put such posts up on a regular basis leading up to your launch. This way, you are giving people value by showing them that you know what you're talking about, you know your stuff and they can see that there's going to be some good content in the book that is going to deliver value for them. Since they can see they are getting value from you teaching them, they're going to trust that, through the book, they will have all of your knowledge packaged nicely for them.

So you need to be able to show that in your pre-launch. Make sure that as you get closer to the launch date, those communications become much more consistent, much more frequent and focussed on driving people to be there for launch day.

Communicate your launch expectations

In your launch support group, make sure that you communicate clearly your expectations and instructions on what they have signed up to do. Talk about the strategy to be a best-seller and that you need them all in on the buy on that first day. Make it clear that no one is obligated to buy if they don't want to and that they can leave the group if they are not willing to support you on the day. You just need people in the group that you can rely on to do what they promised. This is why the daily posts and showing the value in the book is so important.

You can also give them some kind of free bonus as a sign of your appreciation.

CHAPTER 8

FORMAT YOUR BOOK

In this chapter, I'm going to cover the technical aspects of formatting your book correctly.

This is an important part of the book launch to take note of because you need to do what you need to do, not what I did. My first launch was quite painful because I was not clear on the file formats needed nor the distribution aspects. While my print book was fine, my Kindle e-book was formatted incorrectly and it took me a week of communication with Kindle Direct Publishing (KDP) to put it right. This cost me severely in terms of time and in sales as I was not able to advertise around the launch date because I did not want to push the wrongly formatted version to cold traffic.

I don't want that to happen to you, so follow these next steps closely.

Formatting your book file for KDP

KDP has very strict requirements for ensuring that your book is formatted in a way that is compatible with Kindle processes. This applies both for the e-book version and the print version.

You can choose just to launch a print book, or just a Kindle e-book or both. There is also the option for hardback and Audible versions.

For the print version, KDP needs to make sure that the file will convert well to print so you need to follow the exact specifications KDP provides to you regarding file page sizes and margins, gutters and bleeds. This information is fully available on their website. I recommend that you take the time to get familiar with the book formatting requirements before you start to lay out your book.

For the e-book, Kindle readers come in many forms. There are multiple versions of the physical Kindle reader as well as the Kindle app on computer, tablet and mobile phone. Ideally, your file should convert well for all versions. Mine didn't, which is one reason I have written this book. I want others not to have to go through what I had to in order to try to put this right.

So how do you create your book in the correct format?
The easiest and most sure way you can do this is to build the book file on the Kindle Create app. By using this app, you can be more or less sure your book will convert well. I didn't use this first but tried to use a PDF file that was exported from InDesign. I did not realise at the time that this does not convert well.

Next I tried to load the PDF into Kindle Create. This looked really good on all the app views, but wouldn't download on the Kindle Reader so if I had stayed with this version, I would be losing a large portion of my intended audience. That was not the answer.

Finally I rebuilt the book in Microsoft Word in a simple layout using simple fonts and loaded that into Kindle Create. It worked a treat! So do that. Keep it simple.

Another word of warning - if you do upload a PDF file, this is a fixed format file. If you later decide to change the file to one exported from Microsoft Word, which is a flow format, KDP will not allow the swap. So you would need to create a new e-book first and later cancel the first one uploaded, which is another process in itself. This is what happened to me and it took a few days to put right and a few emails to KDP.

So make it easy on yourself and just build your book in Microsoft Word, and upload that into Kindle Create to format it and convert it to the file KDP requires to convert your book into a Kindle book.

You will need to create two files in Kindle Create if you are planning for an e-book and a print book. Follow the instructions in Kindle Create to obtain both files.

To format your book, you will be asked by Kindle Create to identify your chapter titles. Simply check the correct chapter names from the list it gives you and the software will automatically create your Contents page for you.

Use common fonts so that your text converts well. In my first attempt, my header fonts were unusual and, when converted, the letters jumbled together.

Add in your front matter pages (you don't need to include the cover pages as they will be dealt with separately later) and choose the formatting for your sub-headers. Then you are done.

Download your KDP-ready files from Kindle Create and save them on your computer.

You are nearly there!

CHAPTER 9

UPLOAD YOUR BOOK FILES TO KDP

Next, you need to create your book listing in the KDP platform and upload your book content files you just created in Kindle Create.

Create an account on the KDP platform - www.kdp.amazon.com

The building of your book will take place over the following three stages and you will have to repeat the process for each version of the book you want to publish:

1. Book Details
2. Book Content
3. Book Pricing

Book Details

In the Book Details page, you record the title and sub title of your book, and author and publisher names. For the print book, you will also need to enter the ISBN number you have already acquired or apply for one during the set-up process on this page. You do not need an ISBN number for the e-book. You will also be asked to set the publication date. You can choose to publish now or at a future date. If you select a future date, you can also choose whether to allow the book to be pre-ordered. If pre-ordered, people will be able to order your book straight away, but won't receive it into their device or app until the publishing date.

Book Contents

In the Book Contents page, you will upload your cover design file, and your print book/e-book file in separate sections of the page.

For each section, you will be asked to preview and approve the outcome. You will be alerted to any formatting issues and asked to revise and upload the corrected file.

For the print file, once you have no error reports, you are asked to submit the file for further review by the KDP team. This is to double check that the file will work in print. You will receive confirmation or requests for changes within three working days.

Book Pricing

In the Book Pricing page, you will set your prices. This is up to your discretion. For other marketplaces such as UK, etc. KDP will convert the prices for you based on the price you set in the US marketplace.

For the print version, KDP will set a minimum price to ensure that print and distribution costs are covered.

You will also be asked to choose your royalty percentage, set at 35% or 70%.

You can also opt to allow your book to be "borrowed" at no cost to the reader. Borrowing won't be counted in your sales but will be included in your ranking in terms of number of pages read.

Enhanced Distribution

International distribution of your book will be limited to the countries that Kindle lists a marketplace for. You can select Enhanced Distribution for third-party distributors to pick up your book for distribution at additional costs, but this can take eight weeks to come into effect. Buyers in countries not covered by Amazon distribution may not be able to order the print version during this period.

In some countries such as Malaysia, residents won't be able to order your Kindle ebook as the service is not available there.

 As a summary:
- Make sure your book is formatted with the correct margins for Kindle
- Create your file on Microsoft Word first and import into Kindle Create as a PDF for the print book and as a Word doc for the e-book
- Keep your layout simple and use common fonts
- Make your book widely available by choosing each format: e-book, paperback, hardback, Audible and select Enhanced Distribution
- Be aware that some countries can't access Kindle ebooks and some countries can't receive the print version until Enhanced Distribution kicks in

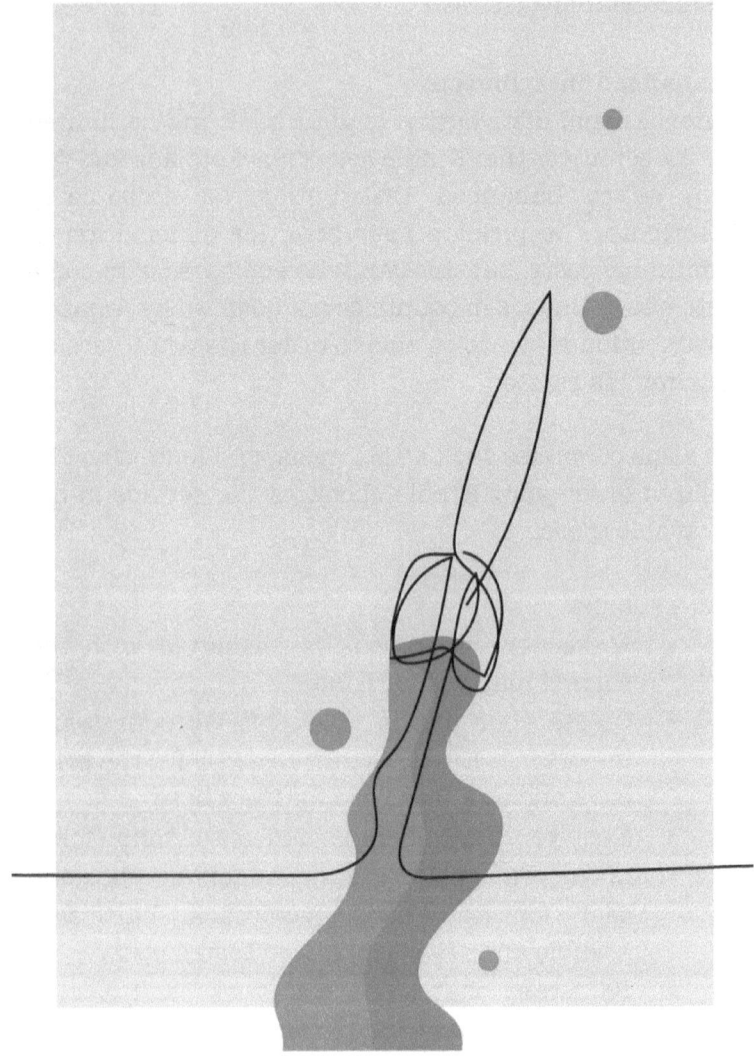

CHAPTER 10

LAUNCH DAY ACTIONS

In this chapter, we will look at how to handle your launch day. As I mentioned earlier on, the week before launch day, you need to really be ramping up your marketing messages to make sure that the people that are supporting you, your launch support group, all know that your book is going to be launched on a particular day.

Communicate hourly

On the day before launch, you need to send them exact instructions of where and how to buy the book. Then throughout launch day, send them repeat instructions with updates as to your book's position on Amazon. The nearer you get to number 1, the more you need to ramp up the urgency for them to get in and buy now. The goal is for them to all buy on the same day, as close as possible in timing to one another.

Keep an eye on your KDP account and check back every hour to see the refreshed position of your book.

Look for where it shows in each category listing and where it shows in the new releases.

Screenshot your climb

Take a screenshot of the evidence as it climbs in the listings and put updates in your social media platforms so that people can see the book is climbing. This will create extra interest because people will begin to see that the strategy really works. You were at number 44 and now you're at number 12. It is getting closer and closer. So you want to create that excitement. You want to create that buzz and awareness, and encourage more people to buy.

You may just need a few more people to go in and buy for your book to hit the number one spot.

Reviews for your book

Another thing you need to be able to tell your people on the launch day is to leave their reviews for your book after three days from the launch day, not on the launch day itself.

A good review, especially from someone who has bought the book on Amazon, will count in Amazon's rankings and it'll also give a lot more trust to people coming in to buy your book cold from ads. When such people come in and see a range of positive reviews from verified purchasers, they are more likely to trust buying the book.

So make sure your buyers review your book after they bought not beforehand. If they review first then buy, the review won't show up as from a verified purchaser. It will still count as a review, but a review from a verified purchaser has a greater impact.

Hopefully by the end of launch day, if there isn't too much competition within your category and there's not too many new launches on the same day, you should quite easily be able to get to number one on Amazon, but of course, there is no guarantee.

Set up your Amazon Author Page

Before you launch your book, take some time to go into your KDP account and set up your Amazon Author Page. This acts like a mini website to promote you and is shown on the sales page for your book on Amazon.

You can add your photos and a bio to promote yourself. Amazon will also feature your book collection as you build it up.

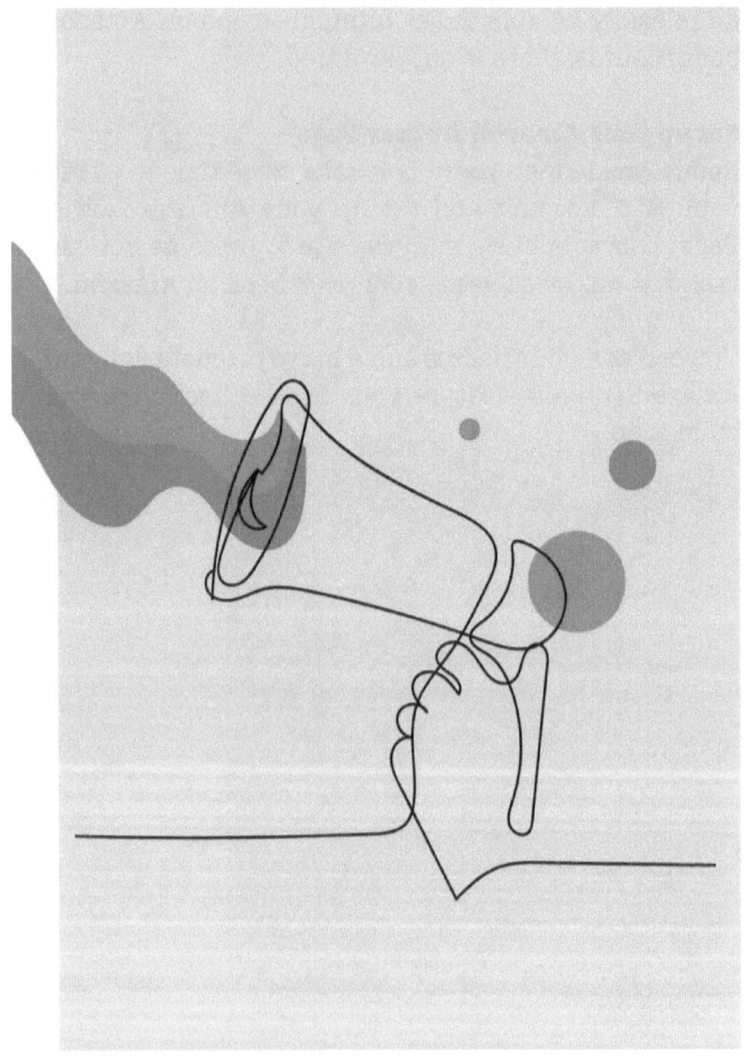

CHAPTER 11

PROMOTE
YOUR BOOK

As I mentioned before, you are probably not going to get rich from sales of your book and the main reason for publication is to help others and be seen as an authority. But it doesn't hurt to be able to sell as many copies as you can because this can be a nice little passive income earner. You build the book once and as long as it remains visible, there is no reason why you can't sell perpetually.

So you need to think about actually promoting the book so that you can get some decent sales from it.

Amazon Advertising Platform
One way to create awareness is through the Amazon Advertising Platform. If you join as a member, you are then able to advertise on the Amazon Advertising platform using their services to advertise.

There are two types of adverts that you can put out.

1. There's the advert where your book shows up on the Amazon platform as a banner that can be clicked and leads to your book sales page.

2. The second kind of ad allows your book to pop up in the Kindle reader itself as a promotion to add the book to the readers' library.

So you've got two types of ads there to consider. You can take out both or one.

Once your ads are live, you can track their progress on the dashboard and see how many impressions your book has made and how many sales.

These ads are extremely easy to set up - just a few minutes to get ads running direct into Kindle devices and on Amazon and that could create a lot more awareness for your book.

You decide how long you want to run the ads for and can renew or cancel at any time.

Facebooks ads
Of course Amazon is not the only way to promote your book. Another way to reach a wider audience is to promote your book on your social media platforms organically and to run your Facebook ads into Facebook and Instagram. You can take potential buyers from the ads to a detailed landing page that gives visitors:

- Detailed insights into the contents of your book
- Reviews from readers
- Call to action to order with a link back to your Amazon sales page

Make your sales page compelling

To make your landing page more compelling, flesh out what they can read on selected pages, for example:

- page 23, you're going to read XXXX,
- page 56 you'll gain powerful insights into XXXXX, etc.

Create a list of about 10 of these to give insights into your book and how it creates value.

The aim of your landing page is to get them interested in the book and to provide a call to action for visitors to click the link to go and buy from Amazon. Don't forget to increase your price from the 99 cents launch offer!

Manage your costs

Be aware as well of the cost of advertising on the platforms you choose. Your costs should be below the income you get from the sales of the book.

Or you can decide that since the sale of the book is good for your reputation and branding, you may be willing to invest in advertising for a short term and chalk it up to a business expense, which is really an investment in your business if you can get a return on investment further down the road. This return can be in the form of exposure, authority building, and brand awareness. There doesn't need to be a monetary return directly from the sales of the book.

Keep in mind too that if you can get momentum on the sale, Amazon will work to promote it and push it as they'll do things to make sure it stays visible if it's proving popular. So once you get that momentum going

I would suggest that you keep it going by running ads and bringing people to the site to buy so that Amazon will keep it visible. This way, you'll get the organic reach on Amazon as well.

In the end, by taking these 11 steps, you will have a book that you should be proud to be able to show to the world.

And perhaps the first of many.

Scan me